EXIT SMART

VOL. 1

EXIT SMART

VOL. 1
Spotlights on Leading Exit Planning Advisors

LEADING EXIT PLANNING ADVISORS

FEATURING

David M. Bastiaans

Gil Bean

Dan Paxton

Gary K. Aldridge

Michael Wildeveld

Craig C. Brigman

Bob Bubser

Austin Collins

Mark W. Boslett

Michael P. Crawford

Copyright © 2022 Remarkable Press™

All rights reserved. No part of this publication may be reproduced, distributed, or transmitted in any form or by any means, including photocopying, recording, or other electronic or mechanical methods, without the prior written, dated, and signed permission of the authors and publisher, except as provided by the United States of America copyright law.

The information presented in this book represents the views of the author as of the date of publication. The author reserves the right to alter and update their opinions based on new conditions. This book is for informational purposes only.

The author and the publisher do not accept any responsibilities for any liabilities resulting from the use of this information. While every attempt has been made to verify the information provided here, the author and the publisher cannot assume any responsibility for errors, inaccuracies, or omissions. Any similarities with people or facts are unintentional.

Exit Smart Vol. 1/ Mark Imperial —1st ed.
Managing Editor/ Shannon Buritz

ISBN: 978-1-954757-23-3

Remarkable Press™

Royalties from the retail sales of "**EXIT SMART Vol 1: Spotlights on Leading Exit Planning Advisors**" are donated to the Global Autism Project:

The Global Autism Project 501(C)3 is a nonprofit organization that provides training to local individuals in evidence-based practice for individuals with autism.

The Global Autism Project believes that every child has the ability to learn, and their potential should not be limited by geographical bounds.

The Global Autism Project seeks to eliminate the disparity in service provision seen around the world by providing high-quality training to individuals providing services in their local community. This training is made sustainable through regular training trips and contiguous remote training.

You can learn more about the Global Autism Project and make direct donations by visiting **GlobalAutismProject.org**.

Contents

A Note to the Reader ix

Introduction xi

David M. Bastiaans 1

Gil Bean 11

Dan Paxton 23

Gary K. Aldridge 39

Michael Wildeveld 49

Craig C. Brigman 67

Bob Bubser 77

Austin Collins 91

Mark W. Boslett 103

Michael P. Crawford 115

About the Publisher 123

A Note to the Reader

Thank you for obtaining your copy of "EXIT SMART Vol. 1: Spotlights on Leading Exit Planning Advisors." This book was originally created as a series of live interviews on my business podcast; that's why it reads like a series of conversations, rather than a traditional book that talks at you.

From dozens of interviews, my team and I have personally chosen the best of the series to feature in this book. We chose these professionals because they have demonstrated that they are true advocates for the success of their clients and have shown their great ability to educate the public on the topic of exiting businesses.

I wanted you to feel as though the participants and I are talking with you, much like a close friend or relative, and felt that creating the material this way would make it easier for you to grasp the topics and put them to use quickly, rather than wading through hundreds of pages.

So relax, grab a pen and paper, take notes, and get ready to learn some fascinating insights from our Leading Exit Planning Advisors.

Warmest regards,

Mark Imperial

Publisher, Author, and Radio Personality

Introduction

"**EXIT SMART Vol. 1: Spotlights on Leading Exit Planning Advisors**" is a collaborative book series featuring leading professionals from across the country.

Remarkable Press™ would like to extend a heartfelt thank you to all participants who took the time to submit their chapter and offer their support in becoming ambassadors for this project.

100% of the royalties from this book's retail sales will be donated to the Global Autism Project. Should you want to make a direct donation, visit their website at **GlobalAutismProject.org**

DAVID M. BASTIAANS

DAVID M. BASTIAANS
Conversation with David M. Bastiaans

David, you are an attorney with Wolcott Rivers, PC. Tell us about your work and the people you help.

David M. Bastiaans: My first profession was a CPA, which I did for approximately four years in Boston, MA, and Washington, DC. I began practicing as an attorney in the Washington, DC area until June 1998, when I joined Wolcott Rivers, P.C. in Virginia Beach. Although I maintain my CPA license, I work as an attorney and advisor to my business clients. I focus my practice on helping business owners with business planning and helping them look at their business differently to build a business they can sell in the future. So we talk a lot about transferable value. In addition to business planning, I also do estate planning, primarily for business owners, because the two plans need to come together.

What are business owners' most significant concerns when they reach out to you?

David M. Bastiaans: Most of their concerns are misinformation and being overwhelmed by the entire process. I don't focus on the "succession" or the "exit." I focus on the business owner. The business is there to serve the owner's goals and objectives. I educate my clients that they need to look at their business as an asset, not an income-producing investment. I want them to create something they can grow and build transferable value. So by doing that, I get their mind off of succession and exit planning. But at the end of the day, I want them to have what I call the "Freedom of Choice." The "Freedom of Choice" is when the owner has an optimally run business and can choose to continue to operate it because they enjoy the business still or sell or exit because the optimal business is at its highest value.

Are there common myths and misconceptions in the world of business ownership?

David M. Bastiaans: One that I hear all the time is "make your key employee an owner." I don't subscribe to that philosophy. I think owners need to have a purpose. If we're going to offer ownership, it's got to be with a purpose. Owners should not offer ownership just because they are worried a key employee will leave, and they shouldn't add them to their succession plan without even considering what that means. Will the employee have the aptitude to be an owner? Do they even want to be an owner? There are other ways to retain key employees without offering ownership.

The other aspect is that owners become overwhelmed thinking about their options. Every time you get in your car, you know where you begin and where the destination will be. If you use one of the popular direction or map apps, the app will reroute you when there is a problem from the original direction. It is no different from helping business owners with their planning. The key is to have a plan, whether it is five year or ten year - have a plan. But you need to be flexible and change the plan when needed. I am currently working with a client who went from considering selling the business to key employees to now considering selling to a third party. I educate my clients on the pros and cons of these options for exiting or succeeding from the business.

How soon should business owners be thinking about an exit plan?

David M. Bastiaans: From inception, a business owner should think about creating something they can grow, creating transferable value, and finally selling. For seasoned businesses, I advise owners to start thinking about their options five years before selling to improve the business and sell at its optimal state. I just met with a young man who is starting his business from the ground up, and I am helping him do it in a way that will give him an investment to transfer in the future. You hear many people say, "Start with the end in mind," however, I don't see a lot of folks doing that. They focus on running the business but don't really have the end in mind. You have to set goals, objectives, and mile markers. Are you achieving those mile markers? You have "Freedom of Choice" if you are reaching those mile markers. Do you exit? Or do you continue down this path? If you don't have an end goal in sight, how will you know when you get there? So it would be best if you had an end goal, whether it is a sale to your employees or a third party. If it doesn't work out, you can shift gears and go in a different direction.

What mistakes do you help your clients avoid?

David M. Bastiaans: The primary one is jumping into something without understanding it. I'm an educator at heart. I've been an adjunct faculty at a local university here for several years. That's my approach in my practice. I want my clients to feel comfortable and understand the overall transaction. So, I use flowcharts and tools to help break everything down. Let's face it; legal documents are not the easiest documents to read. So often, owners enter into something hoping it's what they want, but they don't understand it fully.

David, what inspired you to get started in this field?

David M. Bastiaans: I've been practicing law for 20+ years, and probably after the last 15 or 16 years, my focus has always been on business owners. I was doing shareholder buy/sell agreements to protect the owners from triggering events, and I felt there was a missing component. It was just a transfer amongst owners, but there is so much more to it. So with my CPA and my legal background, I wanted to go into more than exit planning strategy, more of a succession planning strategy. Closely held businesses just don't have the luxury of being able to sell on the open market. So they need to have a plan.

Is there anything else you would like to share?

David M. Bastiaans: All professionals need to be involved with this process. No one professional can provide everything from beginning to end. You need your CPA, attorney, and financial advisor in the room with you and everyone on the same page. One person needs to quarterback that whole scenario or planning engagement. Ensuring that everyone on the team is informed is a key component to the successful transition and succession of a business.

How can people find you, connect with you, and learn more?

David M. Bastiaans: My website for succession planning is www.theoneboss.com. That is where I focus on business succession and business planning as part of my practice. I'm also on my firm's website, Wolcott Rivers, PC, www.wolcottriversgates.com.

The content of this chapter shall not be construed as legal advice on any subject matter but intended for general purposes only and the opinions of David M. Bastiaans. You should seek legal counsel in your jurisdiction prior to acting on any information contained in this chapter.

DAVID M. BASTIAANS, CPA, ESQ., LL.M.

BUSINESS TRANSACTIONS
WOLCOTT RIVERS, PC

As an attorney and CPA, David M. Bastiaans has spent his career focused on assisting businesses and individuals in achieving their strategic goals or helping them solve challenges that may stand in the way of these goals. David has a saying, "If you are not planning, you are reacting!" This proves true for most people in both business and in life. There are those who make things happen, and for others, things happen to them. Mr. Bastiaans' practice concentrates on estate planning, business solutions, and succession or exit planning. David's training as an attorney and CPA, combined with his advanced degree from the University of Alabama School of Law (LL.M – Business Transactions), uniquely qualifies him to assist business owners in realizing their personal and professional goals. He has successfully completed the training offered by the Exit Planning Institute. David works with business owners to attain the "Freedom of Choice" – the point at which the business owner can decide to sell or exit at an optimal value or decide to continue with the business in its optimal state.

EMAIL:
bastiaans@wolriv.com

PHONE:
757-554-0242

WEBSITE:
www.theoneboss.com

LINKEDIN:
https://www.linkedin.com/in/davidmbastiaans

GIL BEAN

GIL BEAN

Conversation with Gil Bean

Gil, you are a partner with ExitSmarts. Tell us about your work and the people you help.

Gil Bean: ExitSmarts is the first company to offer a complete process for business transition. It addresses the planning part of transition and the execution - or implementation - part. We create the plan; we implement the plan - it's as simple as that. Of course, we work directly with business owners, but we go well beyond that by also working with the professionals who advise them. Our Business Transition Coaches are professionals from wealth management, financial planning, exit planning, accounting, insurance, and other disciplines. We empower our coaches to do as much of the business transition process as they want to do or can do. We do the rest.

What common concerns do owners have about selling their businesses?

Gil Bean: I think most business owners are overwhelmed by the idea of selling. They don't know what pieces of the puzzle have to be considered, let alone how they fit together. Most owners have specific concerns based on things they've read or heard, but very few of them have an appreciation of the overall process. That makes sense when you think about it because they have spent so much time building their businesses that they haven't had much time to think about leaving them. When they start to work with us, they're usually shocked when we discuss things they didn't know about or hadn't thought about.

What questions should owners ask themselves as they plan to exit their businesses?

Gil Bean: At the highest level, they should be thinking about five questions: When do they want to sell? To whom do they want to sell? How much do they want or need to make from the sale? What does their transition look like? I left the fifth question for last because it's the most important. Why do they want to transition out of their business? *Why* is critically important because we already know that at least 75% of business owners who sell will regret it within a year of leaving their businesses. That percentage wouldn't be so high if owners knew why they wanted to leave their businesses in the first place.

What types of things should owners think about as they consider moving on to the next chapter in their lives?

Gil Bean: There are three things an owner has to look at when considering a transition: their personal plan, financial plan, and business plan. Although they influence each other, they are actually three very separate things. Sometimes an owner is very clear about the business plan for transitioning but not as clear about the personal or financial plans. When one plan takes precedence over the other two, the imbalance can work against the business owner.

What are some pitfalls that can sabotage a successful exit?

Gil Bean: There are many things, but I would have to point to preconceived ideas on the business owner's part. They may be predisposed to receive a certain amount for the business, but that amount is actually more than the business is worth or less than it could be worth. Or an owner may be focused on transitioning in a predetermined amount of time - six months, for example - when it may be much more advantageous to improve the business and sell it in two to three years. Owners base their preconceptions on things they've read or heard, but those things aren't always accurate, and they might not pertain to an owner's specific situation.

Gil, what inspired you to get started in this field?

Gil Bean: I've been fortunate to have a diverse business career, working with global enterprises and small businesses. I can't say that I've seen it all, but I've seen a lot of it. I spent two years as an implementer of a business operating system called EOS, which really helped me understand the challenges the small business owner faces. During that time, I met Dan Paxton, who eventually invited me to join him at ExitSmarts. Everything just came together, allowing me to use much of what I had learned from different business experiences. I have always been a listener, and there are few disciplines where listening is more important than helping business owners affect successful transitions.

What do you want most from your work with business owners and their advisors?

Gil Bean: I want to prosper, of course. That probably goes without saying. But most of all, I want an opportunity to listen to what they have to say and then apply what I've learned to help them meet their goals and objectives.

How can people find you, connect with you, and learn more?

Gil Bean: Our website is www.exitsmarts.com. My email address at ExitSmarts is gil@exitsmarts.com, and my mobile number is (484)431-3181. I'm always happy to talk with business owners, advisors, or anyone invested in helping owners affect successful business transitions.

GIL BEAN, CEPA

PARTNER
EXITSMARTS

Gil's business career prepared him well for his role as a Partner at ExitSmarts, and even though he would like to take credit for orchestrating that outcome, he can't. Serendipity played its part.

All but two years of Gil's career have been in technology sales. The early years focused on product sales with companies like IBM and CompuServe, but he eventually shifted to the problem-solving aspect of technology with companies like Cullinet, JD Edwards, and SAP. He counts himself as fortunate to have worked with some of the most noteworthy entrepreneurs in the history of enterprise software.

In 2018, Gil became an EOS Implementer, working with business owners and nonprofit executives to improve the way their companies and agencies operate. During his initial EOS training, Gil met and became friends with Dan Paxton, who eventually invited Gil to join him at ExitSmarts. Again, serendipity played its part. Now Gil and Dan work with a third partner – Ross Trahan – to help business owners and their closest advisors affect successful business transitions.

Gil is a graduate of Bowling Green State University, where his studies in Journalism and English somehow landed him a position as a technical writer with IBM. More serendipity. He lives in Galloway Township in southern New Jersey with his wife, Deborah, and he wouldn't hesitate to tell you that meeting her was, without question, the most serendipitous event of his life.

His intense interest in history – and especially the history of indigenous people in North America – culminated in a historical novel published in 2014. Writing, horticulture, and hiking are the three passions of Gil's personal life. As the business owners and advisors who work with ExitSmarts will undoubtedly acknowledge, he doesn't do anything he's not passionate about.

EMAIL:
gil@exitsmarts.com

PHONE:
(484)431-3181

WEBSITE:
www.exitsmarts.com

LINKEDIN:
www.linkedin.com/in/gilbean

DAN PAXTON

DAN PAXTON

Conversation with Dan Paxton

Dan, you are a founder of ExitSmarts. Tell us about your work and the people you help.

Dan Paxton: ExitSmarts has created a business transition system that helps Advisors define the role they want to play in the business transition world, and then we do the rest. We call it the Business Transition System, or BTS. Transition doesn't necessarily mean transitioning out of the business. Some transitions are for the purpose of making a business more valuable, easier to operate, more efficient, more fun, less owner time, or more profitable. So, we've developed a front-to-back system that helps business owners create a transition plan and, most importantly, implement that plan.

A foundational principle of the transition planning process is a multi-Advisor process with each type of Advisor specialist doing their part. Accordingly, throughout the development of BTS, we talked with hundreds of advisors - accountants, lawyers, business value builders, brokers, wealth managers, financial planners, and insurance brokers - who all wanted to participate in this space, each according to their own specialty. Many became accredited to do transition planning. But when they tried to begin their own business transition practices, they quickly realized that there was no existing process to define what they would do or how they would work together with other Advisors to accomplish the objectives of their Business Owner clients.

The "missing link" was a process, and an Advisor role, to coordinate all of the needed specialist Advisors in an effort to develop and implement a transition plan for the Business Owner. BTS defines the role – the Business Transition Coach – and the process for all Advisors to follow in doing their parts of creating and implementing the transition process for the Business Owner. Summarily, at ExitSmarts, we use the comprehensive Business Transition System to both (1) work directly with our own Business Owner clients and (2) to help other Advisors to be able to work together for the benefit of their own clients.

Is exit planning "top of mind" for business owners?

Dan Paxton: The simple answer is NO, and the reasons are numerous. Successful business owners are great entrepreneurs. They've built businesses making lots of money. They are the business, and the business is them. The business is their life, their definition, and they rarely stop to think about not being in the business they created – their baby. And you cannot really blame them – life is good being a successful business owner.

Most business owners only begin to think about exiting as they progress in age or if they become subject to one of the 5Ds – disability, divorce, disagreement, dissolution, or death. The result of this non-attention to transition is that Business Owners often wait until it is too late to execute successful transitions, and then primarily, bad things happen. If Business Owners knew the facts about successful transitions, they would become way more proactive. The data reveals that only about 20% of all businesses that come on the market for sale do, in fact, successfully sell. That is a very scary statistic and is due mainly to not planning for transition.

What are the most common reasons for businesses to go unsold?

Dan Paxton: First and foremost, as alluded to above, almost everybody waits too long to begin planning, if they do any planning at all. Industry wisdom is that successful transitions usually require at least three and as many as seven years to execute. It should be no surprise that a business not ready for sale will probably not get sold. I always draw the comparison of selling a home. We all know that we have to get the home ready for sale, and the more ready the home is, the higher the price it will sell for. Most Business Owners fall prey to the common notion that having the business ready for sale is all about their bottom line, and that is simply not the case. In reality, somewhere between 60-80% of business value is based on the intangible assets rather than the prime tangible asset of the bottom line. The reality is that a business prepared for transition (intangible assets strong) is a less risky business to purchase. The significant intangible assets are management and people, processes and systems, customer relationships, etc. Purchasers pay more for a business as the associated risks are minimized. Each purchaser has a top-end tolerance for how much risk they will accept. The more the associated risk, the less the purchaser's price is always the case. The biggest and most important intangible asset (think, how much risk are we talking about) is management – as in how does the business operate in the absence of the owner.

For example, I had a client in the high-end design/remodel business with a business grossing $2MM and a bottom line of $600K – not a bad business. The client was beyond shocked when I told her that her business had no current value because the business was 100% her, her name, her involvement, her reputation, and a purchaser could not replace that when she departed. (Translate: really high risk of business continuation without the marquee player.) That is certainly one example of the importance of intangible asset value (or, in this case, no value) and its impact on the sales process.

When should business owners start thinking about an exit plan?

Dan Paxton: It is never too early. In fact, there is business wisdom that says that you should start thinking about your exit when you first start a business. The preparedness requirements come into focus when you change positions and imagine that you are the potential buyer. Yes, you want a financially healthy business. Still, you also want one that has strong intangible assets (as mentioned above) - ongoing management, a defined operating system, documented processes, customers and vendors not married to the exiting owner, a healthy internal culture, and more. Unless the business had been intentionally prepared along these lines, you would be a skeptical buyer or a buyer not wanting to pay top dollar.

The preparedness point cannot be emphasized enough unless the business has some unique technology or hard-to-copy product or service, preparedness rules. The statistic above about only a 20% success rate in business sales is almost entirely about not being prepared. And this statistic will become even more challenging in the next five to ten years. Because such a high percentage of businesses are owned by Boomers, and those Boomers want to get out now or soon, there will actually be 15 times more businesses for sale than at any point in history. Combined with a decreasing purchaser base (GenXers without sufficient money to make business purchases and Millennials without the desire to work like the Boomers have), it is an understatement to say that ONLY THE BEST PREPARED WILL SUCCESSFULLY TRANSFER.

Dan, you mentioned creating a system for other professionals such as CPAs, attorneys, and accountants. What did things look like before they had an ExitSmarts system to guide them?

Dan Paxton: This is such an excellent question and one that gets at the heart of why the Exit Planning or Business Transition industry has been stuck in the mud. To clarify this, I need to point out that I am talking about the industry as it relates to the nearly 95% of all privately owned businesses in the United States that are under $20MM in revenue. Transition services for this sector have basically not developed. On the other end, larger businesses – the top 5% - are covered by the M&A and Private Equity firms who totally have their act together and can perform all of the functions necessary for a sale. So these comments are about the service void for the 95%.

I mentioned earlier that there are a lot of Advisors wanting to play in this market – mainly because they see that their Business Owner clients need this help, and they want to provide that help so that they can hold onto their clients. If they cannot help, the competing Advisor down the road may be able to, which can lead to losing the client – immediately or over time. Advisors wanting to play in this market understand that they need to work together with other (non-competing) Advisors to affect a successful transition. And that is where the problems begin. There is simply nowhere in the industry that you will find a roadmap or process for these Advisors to work together. The result is a bunch of well-intended Advisors, each in their own silo. The resulting situation is challenging for both Advisor and Business Owner. When Advisors don't have a process to play together, the Business Owner is left with having to figure out how to connect the dots – what do I need and from whom do I get it...and there is a big assumption here that the Business Owner has an idea of what help they need in the first place. Hence my comment about the industry being stuck in the mud.

It took us a long time to dissect what was really going on and what was needed to fix it. The industry has long referred to a quarterback position as someone who would lead the Business Owner through the process. The thought is that basically any Advisor wanting to work with their Business Owner clients would perform quarterback duties along with the part of the overall process in which they specialize and then work with other Advisors to do their part. Simple enough, but full of problems. What all is included in being the quarterback? What does the overall plan look like? Who is responsible for developing the overall plan? And assuming that the Advisor understands the significance of intangible assets, how do those get addressed? Where do my responsibilities end, and do another Advisor's responsibilities begin? We sort of understand what we are trying to accomplish with the Business Owner, but where is the HOW to do that? And on and on.

Finally, we uncovered what now seems like a pretty simple solution. The quarterback role that the industry talked about had never been defined; it was always mixed in with the overall process. Our simple realization is that there needs to be a defined quarterback role that understands the entire process and guides the Business Owner through the process. We call this role the Business Transition Coach, or BTC.

The BTC process begins with educating the Business Owner about the need for business transition planning and how the whole process works. The BTC needs to have and understand an entire front-to-back process for business transition – what is needed from different Advisor types for each Business Owner situation. The process the BTC uses needs to include both business transition plan development AND business transition plan implementation. The BTC becomes the Business Owner's wingman, confident, and most trusted Advisor throughout the process.

In addition to performing the BTC role, the BTC Advisor can also play other roles in the overall process. For example, suppose the BTC is a financial planner. In that case, the BTC can do the financial planning required in the overall process and coordinate the rest of the overall process with other Advisors. If the BTC is an accountant, the BTC could also do the accounting and perhaps the tax work and coordinate the rest with other Advisors. So, any Advisor type can become a BTC so long as they have an entire process AND other Advisors who understand the process and their part in it.

In fact, and this is likely my most important statement, any Advisor desirous of playing in the Transition Planning or Exit Planning world with the intent of being or becoming the most trusted Advisor to their Business Owner clients MUST, at a minimum, play the BTC role...and they can play more than that as fits their specialty, but they must always be the BTC.

Dan, what inspired you to get started in this field?

Dan Paxton: It's a really interesting evolution. I was an implementer of the EOS (Entrepreneurial Operating System) that emanates from the book Traction. One day out of the blue, I was invited to lunch by a banker who had just completed training as an Exit Planner. He wanted to seek my involvement in his developing Advisor network as a business value builder because that is what I did. In less than half an hour, bells were going off in my head as he described the overarching concept of Exit Planning.

I realized that many of my Business Owner clients had talked about exiting, but the work I was doing with them was focused on the business needs, not the Business Owner's needs. This may seem like a small difference, but it is actually huge. We focused on what was best for the business but were not paying attention to the owner's personal transition needs or the financials to support those needs. I could discuss this difference for hours, but let me just throw out one related statistic. Studies have found that a full 75% of business owners are unhappy with their transition just one year after the transition itself – for many different reasons. There are a ton of layers to this statistic, but in the end, proper planning had not taken place for all of these Business Owners to be disappointed just a year later.

As I processed all of this, I quickly realized that I wanted to be able to help Business Owners with their individual personal goals and transitions – not just their business goals - so I "went back to school" and received accreditation from both of the Exit Planning accrediting bodies: BEI and EPI. Now, all of my work with business owners is grounded in the basic principle of Exit Planning that ALL of my work focuses on helping Business Owners accomplish their foundational objectives: what do you want to do; when do you want to do that; how much will it cost to do that. And this work begins with helping the Business Owner arrive at these objectives in the first place – a significant job all by itself.

How can people find you, connect with you, and learn more?

Dan Paxton: Our website is www.exitsmarts.com. You will find all of our contact information there. We love talking with Business Owners and Business Advisors.

DAN PAXTON, CEPA, AExP, FORMER EOS IMPLEMENTOR

FOUNDER
EXITSMARTS

Dan is the founder of ExitSmarts, the creator of the Business Transition System - a comprehensive Business Transition system built specifically for businesses <$20MM(ish) in revenue. BTS includes both Transition Plan Development and the often-missing Transition Plan Implementation (which includes business value building). In addition to working directly with Business Owners, ExitSmarts works with other Advisors helping them to define and perform their own roles with their Business Owner clients, while ExitSmarts provides the balance of services – resulting in a total transition solution for Business Owners.

ExitSmarts™ was created because of the massive business exits coming in the 2020s and beyond caused by aging Baby Boomers. Specifically, ExitSmarts addresses two significant marketplace voids: (1) there are NO realistic or affordable Transition Planning solutions for Main Street Business Owners: (2) there are no value-building solutions for these same businesses......and successful transition is all about business value.

EMAIL:
dan@exitsmarts.com

PHONE:
815-790-9007

WEBSITE:
www.exitsmarts.com

GARY K. ALDRIDGE

GARY K. ALDRIDGE

Conversation with Gary K. Aldridge

Gary, you are the founder of Aldridge Valuation Advisors in Nashville, Tennessee. Tell us about your work and the people you help.

Gary K. Aldridge: I teach business owners and CEOs how to maximize the value of their businesses. We typically work with businesses under $10 to $20 million in revenue, a perfect sweet spot that applies to any industry or location. That is our target market.

How prepared are owners when it comes time to sell their businesses?

Gary K. Aldridge: Generally, they are not prepared at all. Data from the Exit Planning Institute says that 10 trillion dollars will change hands over the next ten years. But less than half of those business owners have any transition plan whatsoever. Whether it will be a sale internally or externally, they haven't done any planning at all.

What are the primary concerns of business owners when they first reach out to you?

Gary K. Aldridge: They don't have a plan, and they don't know what they need or when they need it. Most of them don't even know their starting point. So I begin my process by finding out where they are today and where they need to be tomorrow. For example, a client came to me recently and said, "Gary, I need to walk away with X dollars when I sell; after broker fees, attorney fees, CPAs, taxes, debt, and everything. I need to walk away with X amount of dollars. I want to do that in five years." That's a perfect scenario. When we start with where he is today, we can see where the gap is, how much time we have, and the target. Now, I help him work from A to Z to get there. So that's a perfect situation for him and me.

How early should owners start preparing for the sale of their business?

Gary K. Aldridge: Start today. Even if you aren't planning on selling today, it takes a long time to move the needle on value. You never know when the right buyer is going to come along. I worked for an employer several years ago who got calls from people wanting to buy all the time. Finally, someone called him and said, "Just tell me what you want for the business." My employer threw out a high number, and the guy said, "Fine, let's go." You can't control the timing, and it takes a while to get there, so start planning now. Three to five years before your desired sell date is generally a good horizon. When I have clients who want to sell in 18 months and want to know how to ramp up sales, it can be hard to do in that amount of time. It's hard to increase sales, get expenses in order, and change processes in 18 months.

How do you increase the value of a business? What levers are you pulling?

Gary K. Aldridge: People start with the numbers, which is a natural place to start. But when you're talking numbers about revenue and expenses, that's growing value by addition.

I want to focus on people, processes, and technology. That's more of a multiplication type. You get a lot more bang for your buck if you have the right people in the right seats and processes in place. Processes and technology are critical whether your business is service-oriented, manufacturing, hospitality, or any other industry. Case in point, I worked with a client whose value was about $700,000 to start. Three years later, we got it to around $4 million. So that's the right direction. That is what I mean by moving the needle on value.

Statistics show that 80% of businesses that go on the market never sell. What are the primary reasons for this?

Gary K. Aldridge: Many businesses aren't even sellable, often because the business is too dependent on the owner. If you take the owner out of the equation, there's really nothing left.

The biggest reason I find is called the "value gap." The seller thinks his business is worth X, but the buyer is only willing to offer Y, and there's a significant gap between the two. So a sale won't happen. Often, the sellers are misinformed or have a lack of understanding about what their business is actually worth.

We're just coming out of a pandemic. Is this a good time to buy and sell businesses? What have you seen in your market?

Gary K. Aldridge: There's a lot of cash chasing good businesses. It's a great time to sell, and the market is really hot. Other business brokers I interact with are always looking for good businesses that fit their particular portfolios. So there's a lot of activity going on right now, and it's an excellent time to buy and sell.

Gary, what inspired you to get started in this field?

Gary K. Aldridge: I have a passion for value. For me, it's just like a scavenger hunt, like digging for gold. I enjoy poring over financials and getting to know the business owner. What's important to them? What do they want? What do they need? Much of my job is to ask questions and listen. But I love the chase. I love the hunt for value.

Is there anything else you would like to share?

Gary K. Aldridge: I want to reiterate to start now. Start now, even if you don't plan to sell for five, ten, or twenty years. The first step is changing your mindset from a seller to a buyer. You need to look at your business as a buyer, which will help you be more objective about it and think about what changes the buyer would want to make. If you go ahead and make those changes, you will increase the value of your business.

How can people find you, connect with you, and learn more?

Gary K. Aldridge: My website is www.garyaldridge.com. You can contact me by email at gary@garyaldridge.com. I've also developed an online course at www.leveragingyou.com, and it's incredibly economical.

GARY K. ALDRIDGE, CPA, CVA, CFE, CEPA

FOUNDER
ALDRIDGE VALUATION ADVISORS

Gary K. Aldridge, MBA, CPA, CVA, CFE, and CEPA, has over 30 years of experience as a CFO or senior financial executive in privately-held businesses, including the following industries: Telecommunications, Hospitality, Non-Profit, Manufacturing, Fabrication, Distribution, Solar Energy, Financial Services, and Healthcare. These companies and clients range from $300k to $100 million in annual revenues.

Aldridge graduated from the University of Mississippi with a BBA in Banking and Finance and the University of Alabama with an MBA, with a concentration in accounting.

Aldridge is licensed as a Certified Public Accountant in Tennessee. He is also a licensed Certified Valuation Analyst through The National Association of Certified Valuators and Analysts (NACVA), a Certified Fraud Examiner through the Association of Certified Fraud Examiners (ACFE), and a Certified Exit Planning Advisor (CEPA). He is also a member of the American Institute of Certified Public Accountants (AICPA).

Aldridge is the founder of *"Leveraging YOU!"* an online course filled with content to help small business owners maximize the value of their business. The course can be found at www.leveragingyou.com.

EMAIL:
gary@garyaldridge.com

PHONE:
615-594-9910

WEBSITE:
Garyaldridge.com

Leveragingyou.com

MICHAEL WILDEVELD

MICHAEL WILDEVELD

Conversation with Michael Wildeveld

Michael, you are the founder of Veld Mergers and Acquisitions. Tell us about your work and the people you help.

Michael Wildeveld: We've engaged in over 1,000 transactions since 2003 and entered the exit planning industry in 2015. At that time, we recognized a very specific need for our clients that generated over $500,000 in earnings to take a more holistic approach to their business transition. After all, exit planning is about far more than the amount a company may sell for. It's about how to best enhance our client's business value and then tackle how much of that amount our clients will ultimately retain. Even more importantly, it's about working with clients to evaluate their own highly unique "big picture" and have the necessary exploratory conversations with them to determine if a transition will satisfy their broader personal, retirement, and legacy-related objectives.

In working with our client-partners, we delve into what their optimal post-transition life may look like, and we hope to prepare them to help to deliver on that vision and more. After all, a number of clients aren't selling to sit idle on a beach. Often they have several opportunities and adventures on the post-transition horizon - whether they realize it at the time of sale or not. We've had the luxury of doing this for over 20 years, so we can pre-plan even when others may have blind spots as to what the future holds. With our experience and planning, our clients can capitalize on the institutional wisdom we've now developed and maximize their sales proceeds, the leverage they possess when going down any particular path, and their transition and post-transition options!

Do business owners know where to start when it comes time to sell?

Michael Wildeveld: Business owners rarely know where to begin when it comes time to sell, and therein lies the challenge. Let's face it, one way or another, everyone will exit their business. The Five Ds (divorce, distress, disagreement, disability, and death) may force business owners to sell. For owners, the only question is whether it will be on the owner's terms or somebody else's terms.

The majority of our clients fail to plan. They are justifiably focused on growing their company. After all, their business is a known commodity, and they are experts in it, so it's a pretty comfortable place. On the other hand, exit planning may appear daunting and filled with unknowns. Most clients don't know where to begin or how to effectively go about planning, let alone explore all of their options. However, that lack of preparedness can be extraordinarily costly - financially and otherwise. It may ultimately dramatically reduce the company valuation and available tax mitigation strategies and dictate the types of investors and transition options available. Ideally, a client should start the planning process in the critical one to five years prior to any contemplated transition. They can tremendously benefit from exploring various transition strategies well before that. With that said, it's better to start planning late than not to start at all!

What is the role of an exit planner, and how do you help business owners?

Michael Wildeveld: The exit planner's role is to "quarterback" the exit planning team, which is comprised of professionals from perhaps 10 to 12 disciplines and several sub-disciplines. Core deal team members may include financial planners, insurance brokers, wealth managers, estate planners, bankers, accountants (tax advisors, valuation, audit, qualify of earnings, diligence, real estate appraisal), human resource consultants, "family counselors" (aka dysfunction therapists), business and personal coaches, the company's in-house or external counsel in addition to M&A counsel, with a number more layered on. So one of the jobs of an exit planner is to get all of these Type A personalities to *hopefully* play nice together and maintain focus on the best outcome for the client. But again, the end-game is not necessarily only about selling the company. That's only one potential facet of a plan; we evaluate if a sale even makes the most sense and consider if alternative transition options fit better into the client's desired "life and legacy" goals. It's about taking a holistic approach to help each client achieve their unique "big picture" goals. Fortunately, we have created a system to make the entire process extraordinarily simple and remarkably straightforward.

Are there myths and misconceptions about exit planning?

Michael Wildeveld: Those familiar with exit planning will know that there is nothing but preconceived notions about what it is, what it entails, and lastly, what the most important components of exit planning are. First, every seller focuses on their exit value. They may say, "I want to sell my business for $10 million." They may have some number in their head, but they're not taking into account what they stand to net after capital gains taxes, banker fees, and other deal-related expenses. They also aren't considering the available tax mitigation options and post-sale investment strategies. They rarely appreciate that the various planners may need to prepare the seller and company to participate in several of those strategies before going to market!

Let's assume we have a company doing $2 million in EBITDA. Their friend (who is invariably a business genius since he manages a 7-11) "knows" the company should trade for a five times multiple. As a result, our client focuses on that $10 million top-line number. They reverse engineer what they think the key metric is, which in this case is a 5x sales multiple. They then determine that a $1 ml increase in earnings may net them an additional $5 ml in sale value, and without consulting with their team, they invest a few years and a few hundred thousand dollars to achieve a $15 ml sale. This strategy is fraught with hidden costs and risks. First, assuming the company was actually worth $10 ml, this seller may miss their market window due to an ever-changing economic climate. Next, their market position may have weakened, or worse; they may have mucked up the winning formula with their aggressive pursuit of short-term growth (did they launch a sub-par product, engage in discounted sales, or did the delay allow competition to enter the marketplace?) Finally, their aggressive presale push may have adversely impacted company culture, or they could have lost key employees in the process.

With proper advance planning, that same seller may have netted more out of sale proceeds at a $10 million strike price than they may after they try to grow the company, even if they can sell for $15 million! I've seen examples where sellers net more through substantial charitable gifting than by doing nothing at all (you surely didn't believe that all forms of philanthropy were purely altruistic). The point is if you plan strategically, you can get the same amount of juice without necessarily feeling the squeeze.

Obviously, there's a learning curve associated with understanding the exit planning resources available. I'm on the "inside" of the exit planning fence, and I'm still learning every day! Imagine the case for most of our client's legacy trusted advisors who don't do this every day. They simply cannot be exposed to all of these different fields and strategies because they have no reason to be. As a rule, because of any given practice's licensing and related compliance issues, many advisors can only discuss or promote their company's preferred products and services (which tend to be extraordinarily conservative). The reality is that there is a whole range of transition options and tax mitigation strategies that may be implemented in any given sale. Still, there is no central repository for all of them. Compounding the challenge, many strategies may appear risky (and some genuinely are). At the same time, in other cases, the parties that house the knowledge are competitors and are incentivized not to collaborate with others. If this weren't enough, many of those with the savviest strategies purposely remain off of everyone's radar because they don't trigger unnecessary attention from the taxing authorities, face heightened scrutiny from centers of influence or attract unwanted competition.

To look at how complex this can quickly get if we allow it to, let's say there are 20 core transition strategies. Three of them are those that everyone is familiar with - a traditional sale, an ESOP or sale to your employees, or family succession. That leaves 17 that range from somewhat simple to slightly complicated and even outright exotic (perhaps five of which we've developed or championed). Within those 20 strategies are several non-traditional options that can fulfill an owner's need, however unique. Now combine those 20 with perhaps 40 tax mitigation strategies from tax planners, wealth managers, and attorneys. That means there are 800 combinations or permutations to maximize an owner's transition options that they (and their historic advisors and influencers) are likely completely unaware of. How does anyone go into any transition with any degree of confidence if they are unaware of so many options? Imagine how much leverage and control an owner that doesn't know their options gives up. This may be worse than not knowing their actual business valuation.

Michael, what inspired you to get started in this field?

Michael Wildeveld: I've found that everyone relishes hacks and feeling that they were able to "beat the system." I'm no different.

For example, I married for the first time at 19. My ex-wife and I completed our undergraduate work at Vanderbilt University, and she went on to Vanderbilt Law School. It was already terribly costly in the early 1990s, so I juggled three jobs. I obviously couldn't afford to embrace my passion for exploring the globe during these challenging times, so I had to develop a workaround. I chose my jobs strategically. I chose a paid internship with Prudential Financial (then Prudential-Bache Securities) to learn about securities brokerage and investing. Next, I applied with every major airline in Nashville and landed a job marshaling and loading aircraft for American Airlines and emptying the airplane toilets. Finally, I became a bellman and valet at the Holiday Inn Crowne Plaza. Despite only clearing $5.50 an hour in each job, we were able to fly around the world first-class and stay for $5 a night. Since we could eat, sleep and enjoy in-flight entertainment when flying, it became less expensive to take a short trip to Europe or the Caribbean than to stay home! This was by no means my first "hack," but given my penchant for travel and the sense of freedom that accompanies it, it remains one of my favorites. Prior to this travel hack, I figured out two methods of buying exotic autos on the cheap, beating the Las Vegas casinos at their own game without risk of loss and supplying my high school classmates with unlimited beer at a stellar profit; all before being old enough to drive.

These same types of perfectly legitimate hacks exist when it comes to selling your business. For most of our early years selling companies, we focused on the numerator in the sale equation - the sale price. After implementing our preferred methods to maximize the client's enterprise value (my favorite being to arbitrage an offering's valuation multiples by strategically engineering its size), we learned that even greater rewards might be found when focusing on the denominator in the sale equation. The items in the denominator include those costs that decrease our client's sales proceeds, such as capital gains tax rates, pre and post-tax monies remaining to invest, etc. When we can have a client's tax advisors, investment advisors, financial planners, estate planners, wealth managers, etc., all work in concert with one another towards the client's ultimate objective, an untold number of solid strategies in each category can be engineered. In our role, we can pass our knowledge on to clients (and often their advisors), so they can confidently go into any transition discussion with their eyes wide open once they have explored the options available to them and maximized the value they've created.

Is there anything else you would like to share?

Michael Wildeveld: I have a couple of quick tips for business owners. Number one, you've got to trust the process and go into exit planning with an open mind. There's a great book called "Mindset" by Carol Dweck about embracing an open versus fixed mindset. Many clients have a preconceived notion of how everything "has" to be. They feel they need a traditional sale to a competitor, private-equity group, or large corporation. They also need to receive cash at close to ride off into the sunset properly. Though these requirements may appear attractive at first, they may not be in their own best interest. The reality is that they cannot determine what decisions are in or out of alignment with where they need to be until they have fully assessed the options available to them, created their financial plan, determined what they actually want to do 12+ months post-transition and what they want their legacy to look like.

I'll share the ugly truth about business sales. *Most sellers are ultimately dissatisfied with their exits.* This is no reflection on us. Our clients typically love us and appreciate that we accomplish exactly what they asked us to do in a graceful manner. The challenge is that few of our clients can capitalize on all of the options available because they don't embrace an open mindset when exploring the alternative exit and tax mitigation strategies or don't begin the planning process soon enough. Sadly, there is an entire landscape of possibilities out there that most clients will never actually see. In exit planning, we explore, we strategize, and yes, we plan and then implement. We become force multipliers for the number of options and opportunities available.

How can people find you, connect with you, and learn more?

Michael Wildeveld: Our website is www.veldma.com. We have an Exit Ability Assessment for people to discover where they are in the planning process. You don't have to be a client to find it worthwhile. Anyone can complete it or call us without any obligation for a confidential exploratory discussion.

Rest assured that our goal is not to get prospects into a sales funnel - we feel that's counterproductive to all of us, and it's just not how we're wired. In fact, we often tell potential or existing clients *not to sell* if doing so isn't in alignment with their goals or isn't otherwise in their best interests.

Alternatively, potential clients or their advisors can simply call us if they prefer. It all starts with a conversation ...

MICHAEL WILDEVELD

VELD MERGERS & ACQUISITIONS (M&A) |
THE VELD GROUP (MAIN STREET)

Michael Wildeveld, a high school valedictorian, holds a B.A. in Economics from Vanderbilt University and an MBA from the University of Michigan. Michael actively participates in all leading industry organizations, is a Merger & Acquisition Master Intermediary (M&AMI), an expert witness, and a member of the National Association of Certified

Business Valuators and Analysts (NACVA), the Association for Corporate Growth (ACG) and ProVisors. He holds the following certifications - Mergers and Acquisitions Professional (CM&AP), M&A Advisor (CM&AA), Business Intermediary (CBI), Business Broker (CBB), and Exit Planning Advisor (CEPA).

Michael started Value-Line Maintenance at 18 and turned it into a 35-employee enterprise within a year. After college, he gained blue-chip experience with best-in-class employers. He worked in finance for American Airlines, internal audit for ARCO/British Petroleum, business development for Virgin Entertainment, strategic planning, and buy-side mergers and acquisitions for G.E. Capital Aviation and Universal Pictures. Mr. Wildeveld consulted for Jordan's Queen Noor, government ministries in Jordan and El Salvador, Fred Alger Investment Management, and The Landmine Survivors' Network, a Nobel Peace Prize-winning non-profit. Michael has carried out projects in 19 countries in Africa, Asia, Europe, and South America.

Mr. Wildeveld launched The Veld Business Advisory Group in 2002 with his two best friends since age 14. Though they began as a retainer-based consulting and valuation firm, they launched their business brokerage in 2004 and later their boutique mergers and acquisitions practice to address the substantial challenges their valuation clients with less than $20 million in enterprise value faced when going to market. Since then, the companies have performed over 300 formal and 5,000 informal valuations, participated in over 1,000 sell-side transactions, and achieved an 80%+ success rate versus the 30% industry standard.

Michael is passionate about cultivating disruptive concepts and engages in business service and product launches, acquisitions, and roll-ups where value may be created or valuation multiples arbitraged. Michael has completed a marathon but remains a struggling golfer. On a quest to explore the world, Michael has visited over 130 countries and all seven continents.

EMAIL:
michaelw@veldma.com

PHONE:
310.652.8066

WEBSITE:
www.veldma.com (M&A) | www.theveldgroup.com (Main Street)

CRAIG C.
BRIGMAN

CRAIG C. BRIGMAN

Conversation with Craig C. Brigman

Craig, you are a financial advisor with Edward Jones. Tell us about your work and the people you help.

Craig C. Brigman: I specialize in working with business owners. I help them prepare personally and financially for retirement, exit, or whatever their next adventure will be. We work on their business to ensure it can exit at the highest possible output. We have found that the Local Economic Development Authority and SBA have tons of resources for entrepreneurs just starting out. But the guys who have been in business for up to 30 years have no resources to help them learn how to capitalize on their most significant asset. So we want to make sure they are not only educated but also supported by a team.

When is the best time to start planning an exit?

Craig C. Brigman: Realistically, you want to have a plan in place before one of the 5 Ds happens (death, disability, divorce, disagreement, distress). If any of these occur, you will need to sell quickly, putting you in a bad position. The minute the business is profitable, you should start thinking about an exit plan. Ask yourself, "How do I maximize the value of my business and turn it into real wealth, whether the offer comes unexpectedly or has been planned and in the works for years?"

Are there myths and misconceptions about exit planning?

Craig C. Brigman: There are many misconceptions. I'll give you a couple of examples. Over the last few years, we have asked many business owners about their retirement plans. They typically respond, "I plan to sell my business." But they delay and put it off, and suddenly, they are 68 to 72 years old, unable to continue the day-to-day operations. Now they have to find a buyer. So not only were they not prepared for it, but they also weren't going to get the value they believed was in the business.

Outside of that, we have also found that many business owners have unrealistic expectations about what their businesses are worth. I've heard everything from "ten times the multiple of my gross revenue" to "I will get five to six million dollars for this $100,000 business." So a lot of our job is making sure business owners know what their business is really worth and where they can add value to increase that net worth, so when they exit out and make that sale, they're prepared. Not only do they know their options, but they exit at a higher value, which has a real impact on their long-term future.

What are the pitfalls that prevent business owners from exiting successfully?

Craig C. Brigman: The first one is not being prepared. Part of it is them thinking they will exit out and do exactly what they want, which is often their idealized version of life. For example, I had a client who said, "We will retire and move to Colorado and live on 100 rural acres in a secluded, pastoral experience." Looking at his wife, I could immediately tell that was not her ideal transition. So I asked, "Have you talked with your wife about this? You will go from working 60 to 80 hours a week over the last 30 years to spending 24 hours a day, seven days a week with your spouse." Often the business owner thinks they have the ideal exit pictured, but their spouse has an entirely different viewpoint.

The next issue is being financially unprepared. Business owners sometimes bank on selling the business for several million dollars and riding off into the sunset. Because they've done no real planning ahead of time, they are very disappointed when they don't get the offer they expected. Many business owners just aren't familiar with the process. They go through the process, sell, but then find they weren't personally and emotionally ready to go on and do something else.

Craig, what inspired you to get started in this field?

Craig C. Brigman: I started 15 to 18 years ago when I became an IRS agent. I used to audit companies and business owners up to about $100 million in income. Then I later became a college professor and looked at business and tax situations. As I came into financial advice and financial planning, I found there were no resources for business owners. Over the years of consulting business owners, I found that 80% were unprepared for that transition. They all just believed that they would exit into the sunset with millions of dollars in their saddlebags. And realistically, they were getting offers that were 20% and 30% of that. So we really want to make sure they are emotionally and financially prepared and that the business sale doesn't become the primary means for them moving on. We want the sale to be more like the gravy. So if they've done everything else, when they walk away from that, that's really the icing on the cake. Then they can leave anytime and not fall victim to one of the 5 Ds we discussed.

Is there anything else you would like to share with owners considering exiting their businesses?

Craig C. Brigman: You should consider getting a CEPA (Certified Exit Planning Advisor). They are trained to understand what you are going through and what you expect and can walk you through that process. Then make sure that you're building a good team around you. That team will include not only your CEPA, like me, but a CPA, a business broker, a business banker, and an attorney who handles business transactions. You start to build your team around you and explore the available options.

I also advise my clients to stay engaged. If you're going to add value to your business, you don't do it all at one time. I live by a rule: "It's progress, not perfection." As long as we have some lead time, we can work to add some value to the business and make it the best in class.

In addition, don't underestimate being emotionally prepared to sell your business. Talk about your plans with your spouse, significant other, and family. And then have those honest conversations about going from spending years of your life in the business to being at home. When you are ready to transition and leave, you have a game plan that will be more valuable to you than anything else. While an exit plan doesn't have to be written down, getting those pieces in place is good to help you succeed.

How can people find you, connect with you, and learn more?

Craig C. Brigman: The best way is to connect with me on LinkedIn - Craig Brigman. You will find my office and all of my contact information there. If you need to do something quickly and want to talk through it, I work with clients all over the United States. Feel free to give me a call or message me directly. We're happy to speak with anybody and at least figure out where you are and where you want to be.

CRAIG C. BRIGMAN, CEPA©, AAMS™, CPRC™, CPRS™, CSRIC™

FINANCIAL ADVISOR
EDWARD JONES

Some people say that Craig was born a genius. However, the truth is that he is just a normal guy who works really hard at providing knowledge, experience, and value to his clients. Before becoming a wealth advisor, he was an IRS Agent, auditing small businesses and self-employed taxpayers with up to $100M in income. After leaving the IRS, Craig became a college professor and consultant. As a college professor, he taught thousands of students, was a subject matter expert, and developed content for multiple textbook publishers. Additionally, Craig was a consultant to small to medium-sized businesses helping rebuild and reshape companies to be more valuable and reach the next level. Using all his education and experience, Craig now helps business owners realize the value in their largest asset - their business.

EMAIL:
ccbrigman@gmail.com

PHONE:
540-588-9501

WEBSITE:
https://www.linkedin.com/in/craigbrigman/

BOB BUBSER

BOB BUBSER

Conversation with Bob Bubser

Bob, you are a Wealth Advisor with FPA Wealth Management. Tell us about your work and the people you help.

Bob Bubser: My practice focuses on small to midsize businesses and their owners. Creating a financial plan, establishing goals, and building a roadmap is the foundation of most of my financial relationships. While our team at FPA Wealth Management works with all types of business owners, my experience would be in the distribution sector.

I am a former business owner. My experience started in an auto parts store where I was a stock boy and driver at 16 years old. Over the next few decades, I worked hard and advanced within the company. Fast forward 20 years, and I became an equity partner. We owned 150 stores and bought most of them. We sold the company in 2013 to a Fortune 500 company, and I retired... but I didn't like retirement, so I reinvented myself. And now, I help other business owners in the auto parts industry to prepare for the dubious mental and physical task of selling their businesses. It's a process that isn't easy for most people.

Do owners in the auto industry know where to start when selling a business? What was it like in your experience?

Bob Bubser: In my personal experience in the automotive aftermarket, our company was large. We had several partners, 1,600 employees, and 150 locations. We were the ninth-largest auto parts distributor in the United States. We engaged with many private equity groups when the decision was made that we were ready to exit the business. Our company also spoke with several strategic buyers and ended up selling to one of them.

Business owners are brave, smart, and hardworking people. Too often, they are so focused on their company and working so hard, that thinking about their next step sits on the back burner... often until it is too late. These owners are the best at running a business, but they have never sold one. They have no idea where to start or how to prepare. There's a lot to it. I help owners understand the process, and usher them through an exit plan.

What concerns do business owners have when they reach out to you?

Bob Bubser: "Can I afford it? Mentally I am ready. Where do I start? What can I do to prepare for my eventual exit?" This is a great conversation, because just saying this aloud is therapeutic for a business owner. During follow up discovery meetings, there are hundreds of questions we ask business owners to help them with their concerns and with the preparation. If they have children, are the kids interested in taking over the business? If they are interested, are they ready, and can they afford it? How strong is the management team? Could one of them be a potential buyer of the business? Do you want to work after the sale, and in what capacity?

Especially in today's environment, buyers want your staff to stay on board. Is your staff strong enough to make your company attractive? Have you mentored key people and delegated responsibilities? Is the owner responsible for all the sales growth, making all the operational decisions and single handedly steering the ship?

Most owners understand this, but it is difficult to let go of the reins. If the owner wants to stop working, and *basically is* the business, there won't be much left for a buyer to work with. If the owner doesn't have a strong team in place, he won't get top dollar.

Are there any myths or misconceptions about selling a business?

Bob Bubser: One of the unfortunate misconceptions is some owners of smaller companies think the business is worth a lot more than it's worth. I have always believed that a business is worth what someone is willing to pay for it. There are methods and strategies to prepare your company for the eventual sale. If you run your business like you'll sell it, you will make more money along the way and you will get a higher sale price. You've got to show a profit if you expect someone to pay you a premium price.

How did the recent pandemic affect the auto industry?

Bob Bubser: Interesting question, and I'll tell you why. When the country shut down in late March, the auto parts industry, including the part stores and repair shops, were deemed essential businesses. They stayed open. But the public wasn't driving out to get their cars fixed or going to parts stores. The country was nervous. We didn't know what to expect. For a couple of months, sales tanked by 50% to 80%. Two months later, as people got a little more comfortable, they started coming out of the house and fixing their own cars and, in many cases, having their vehicles repaired at shops. Business started to pick up and quickly began to boom. Since people weren't going to work, they had time to work on their cars. They weren't spending money going out to eat because the restaurants were closed, and they had money to put into their cars.

In the meantime, the PPP program came around, and the intelligent business owners applied for PPP loans, not knowing that things would get better. In some cases, store owners got hundreds of thousands of dollars, maybe a million-plus. By the end of the year, they had a GREAT year. And the next year was their best year ever. The companies didn't have to repay the money if they used it appropriately. This really boosted bottom lines and gave them a real surge in net income which enabled stores to build inventory levels. And all was good.

But part two, owners have been very frustrated with supply chain challenges. There are unprecedented backorders and availability issues. Auto parts stores feel like they cannot give their customers the good service they have always provided. Installer customers who do repairs on consumer vehicles now have to make sure the parts are actually available before they can schedule the work. This has created a notable change in the industry.

Is it a good time to sell a business? What have you seen in your market?

Bob Bubser: It's a great time to sell if you're showing a healthy profit, and most stores are because they are having their best year. Whether you're selling on a multiple of EBITDA or selling your assets with a goodwill number, it's a suitable time. With price increases, your inventory value has gone up considerably. Large strategic buyers want to grow their businesses and are looking for businesses to acquire on the demand side.

Secondly, suppose you have one hundred employees who come to work every day and punch a clock, and a buyer wants to purchase your business. In that case, it's attractive to have the employees already in place, especially since they are trained in the industry. Now more than ever, finding employees is a challenge right now. The answer is yes – it is an exceptionally good time for auto parts stores to sell their companies.

Bob, what inspired you to get started in this field?

Bob Bubser: I got into the financial planning field after I retired. Actually, my wife booted me out of the house within a month - it kind of ruined her routine with me hanging around the house all the time. Honestly, I was itching to get into the field again. Much of the inspiration really came from having the opportunity to work with business owners I knew. I have friends and relationships with people in the industry, and they need help. It's extremely rewarding to help someone do something they can't really do on their own. I'm bringing a lot of value, and my driving force is helping these companies accomplish their goals. I know what kind of help they need. I believe my clients appreciate the advice and support I provide to them during this process.

Is there anything else you would like to share with owners thinking about exiting their businesses?

Bob Bubser: You can search the internet for different people to help you sell your business. I'm a Wealth Advisor, and I bring a lot of business experience and a real-world perspective to a client. I've got a CEPA® designation, a Certified Exit Planning Advisor. This designates me as a specialist in exit planning. I would undoubtedly advise touching base with someone like that. CEPA® Advisors have been extensively trained and often have firsthand experiences such as mine that led them into this field.

How can people find you, connect with you, and learn more?

Bob Bubser: My website is www.fpawealthmgmt.com. You can also reach me by phone at 856-296-3955.

BOB BUBSER, CEPA®, AIF®

WEALTH ADVISOR
FPA WEALTH MANAGEMENT

Bob Bubser brings a unique perspective to FPA Wealth Management. At the age of sixteen, Bob began working part-time at an auto parts store in White Plains, NY. He maintained employment there throughout college and upon graduating from the State University of New York at Oneonta earning a Bachelors Degree in Business-Economics.

Bob advanced to the leadership team and partook in the company's growth from one store in New York to the ninth largest automotive parts distribution company in the United States. As Division President and Equity Partner, Bob spent fifteen years on the Board of Directors. After selling the company in 2013 to a Fortune 500 company, Bob was selected to assist in a three-year transition period.

After this transition period, Bob recognized the need that business owners had for personal financial planning and business succession planning. In 2017 he decided to enter the financial services industry. His background in business gave him a unique ability to understand and relate to clients, especially when it comes to business transition planning. Bob's clients' range in size from mom-and-pop businesses to large corporations with 10,000 employees.

Bob holds various insurance licenses including life, health, disability, and long- term care insurance. In addition, Bob holds a FINRA series 6, 7, 63 and 65, registered with LPL Financial. Bob's financial credentials also include the Accredited Investment Fiduciary® (AIF®) and Certified Exit Planning Advisor (CEPA®) designations.

Bob resides in Randolph, NJ with his wife, Jean, and their black cat Spooky. They have three children and two young grandchildren who call Bob "Choo" and Jean "Mimi." Their family loves to travel, often to far away lands to indulge in the history and culture of different societies. They split their time between New Jersey and Vero Beach, Florida where they love entertaining family and friends.

EMAIL:
bbubser@fpawealthmgmt.com

PHONE:
856-296-3955

WEBSITE:
www.fpawealthmgmt.com

AUSTIN COLLINS

AUSTIN COLLINS

Conversation with Austin Collins

Austin, you are the Founding Principal of Integrated Wealth Advisors. Tell us about your work and the people you help.

Austin Collins: Integrated Wealth Advisors is a Virtual Family Office (VFO) practice. We believe that simplifying all the intersections of life and money creates confidence and time to do what you love. We are known for helping entrepreneurs feel grounded by simplifying the most complex transitions of their lives. Over a third of our clients have made work optional since beginning a relationship with us—many of those through successful exits from their companies. We often work with owners of companies valued between $3 million and $20 million who are considering a full or partial exit in the next five years. These entrepreneurs have created so many opportunities for others, and we believe they deserve clarity, guidance, and support to leverage their own opportunities and manifest the ideal next chapter in their lives.

Our VFO simplifies the intersections of life and money for our clients by leveraging a wide-ranging group of pre-vetted top professionals in disciplines from legal to tax, operations, business, real estate, lifestyle, and even medical. Each client benefits from this network in unique ways, as we build each of them a fully customized professional team. Often their existing team forms the foundation, and we strategically weave in other professionals at the right times for the right reasons. Over time, we leverage innovative tools, technology, and processes to align these experts with our client's objectives seamlessly.

Do business owners know where to start when planning an exit?

Austin Collins: Some do, but they are certainly in the minority. Only 4% of owners have a formal "life after business" plan.* This is a huge part of why a full 75% of owners "profoundly regretted" the decision to sell after one year.* The best place to start when considering selling your business is to define your ideal outcome clearly. Answer this question without talking about the sale price of your company. Dream in detail about what your life will look like after a successful transition. What are you excited about doing next? The intention here is to create something to look forward to and move towards.

A great exercise to help create clarity is the Ideal Week exercise. Take a blank weekly calendar, a full 168 hours, and map out exactly how your time would be spent, after a successful company sale, if you had an absolutely perfect week. When and how much are you sleeping? How are you staying spiritually grounded and physically fit? Who are you spending time with? Are you doing any personal development work? What about hobbies? Are there any time commitments for consulting as a part of the company sale? What projects are creating meaning and fulfillment? What impact are you having on the people around you and in your community? Completing this exercise gives you a target to shoot for. Odds are you will never have a week that looks exactly like the one you created. That's just fine since the real value in this exercise is the clarity and alignment that comes from challenging yourself to define your ideal outcome in advance.

What key factors do owners typically not consider during exit planning?

Austin Collins: The relationship between deal terms and the owner's personal financial future is one often overlooked dynamic that can dramatically improve outcomes. Consider the example of a buyer lowering their price by $1 million based on their findings in due diligence. How does this impact the owner? Many assume the answer is simple: the owner walks away with $1 million less. But the real answer is quite a bit more nuanced. First, assuming a 20% tax rate, the owner walks away with $800,000 less, not a million. But the original question remains unanswered. How does this impact the owner? Money by itself is meaningless. It must be measured against the job it will need to do. In this case, if we assume the owner wants to retire, the impact of $800,000 less can be "measured" in the change to sustainable monthly income. Sustainable income rates are different for everyone. There are many factors to consider, including desired investment risk level, interest rates, and even longevity. Depending on these and other variables, the range of sustainable income from $800,000 might be $2,000 - $2,600/month. How much will this decrease in monthly income impact the owner after the sale? Understanding personal impact gives the owner a powerful lens through which to evaluate the deal terms.

Things often change quickly during negotiations. Staying firmly grounded in post-sale reality during a deal creates clarity to navigate in alignment with what is most important.

How has the recent pandemic affected people in the business community?

Austin Collins: It has definitely forced everybody to become much more adaptable. It has also helped to focus people on thinking creatively about how to create the most sustainable value for their companies. Some industries have obviously slowed considerably more than others, but it certainly hasn't stopped sales of high-quality businesses. We have clients in medicine, technology, engineering, and architecture who have successfully transitioned businesses since the pandemic started.

Austin, what inspired you to get started in this field?

Austin Collins: Business ownership was in my family growing up. My father and stepfather owned architecture firms in Seattle, and they each had very different entrepreneurial operating systems. I saw how different ways of navigating could lead to very different outcomes. It was an opportunity for me to understand the long-term advantages of thinking more strategically and doing better planning. Watching that unfold firsthand every day for over a decade as a kid was a unique and valuable experience.

I started working in my current role as a wealth manager in the mid-2000s, and it became clear very quickly that I really enjoyed supporting and empowering business owners. These entrepreneurs create all kinds of opportunities for other people and a positive ripple effect of value for their communities. They deserve way better outcomes and more support than they typically get, which will, in turn, allow them to have an even more significant impact. It is something that I've always been passionate about since I was young, but that passion definitely evolved in my career as an advisor.

Is there anything else you would like to share with business owners considering exiting?

Austin Collins: Don't underestimate the value of the right transition team! Most owners are unaware of the right team's impact, as 88% have no formal transition advisory team.* That also may explain why 70% to 80% of privately owned businesses on the market don't sell.* Selling your company is a three-dimensional process. It is easy to fall into two-dimensional thinking, focusing only on issues within the business, like management continuity, customer retention, earnings calculations, and valuation multiples. These are critical issues, no doubt, and the deal would likely fall apart if significant time and attention were not dedicated to them. But focusing on the content of the business alone, without thought to the different contexts in which the business exists, often creates deal friction and missed opportunities.

Your company sits at a unique intersection of operational conditions. These conditions include company legal structure, tax profile, industry, geographic location, market conditions, and the personal situations of all key stakeholders, from owners and families to key employees. To have a truly three-dimensional view of your business and of the deal itself as it unfolds, you need top experts in each of these areas to provide insight and guidance on an ongoing basis. The ideal team will vary depending on the business but will often include a CPA, M&A attorney, Investment Banker, Wealth Manager, Value Advisor, and an Executive Coach. One of these professionals should serve as the point person for your team by proactively coordinating the efforts of each professional in alignment with your objectives. If you think that sounds too expensive, don't worry. Each of those professionals should be able to illustrate the ROI of working with them. Share your concerns with them and have an open dialogue. If they are genuinely the right partners, you will resonate with them more as a result of that conversation.

How can people find you, connect with you, and learn more?

Austin Collins: You can connect with me on LinkedIn if you are open to expanding your network. If you would like to reach me directly, my company website is www.integratedwa.com. My digital business card has information about the Integrated Wealth Advisors VFO, in addition to some other projects I'm actively working on: www.austincollins.org. That is the best way to get a feeling for who I am and whether we might resonate well working together.

* Statistics sourced from 2013 Northeast Ohio Chapter of the Exit Planning Institute "State of Owner Readiness" Survey Full Report. By: Chris Cooper, Ohio Employee Ownership Center, Kent State University, and the 2016 "State of Owner Readiness" Updated Survey Results. By: Patrick C. O'Brien MBA, CEPA, PNC Wealth Management, EPI National Advisory Board.

Securities and advisory services offered through Commonwealth Financial Network®, Member www.FINRA.org, www.SIPC.org, a Registered Investment Adviser. Financial planning services offered through Integrated Wealth Advisors, a WA Registered Investment Adviser, are separate and unrelated to Commonwealth.

AUSTIN COLLINS, CEPA®, RICP®, AWMA®, CRPC®, CLTC®

Founding Principal, Certified Exit Planning Advisor
Integrated Wealth Advisors

Austin believes that simplifying the intersections of life and money creates confidence and time to do what you love. He often works with business owners considering a full or partial exit in the next five years. These entrepreneurs have created so many opportunities for others, and they deserve clarity, guidance, and support to leverage their own opportunities and manifest the ideal next chapter in their lives.

EMAIL:
austin@integratedwa.com

PHONE:
425-818-0717

WEBSITE:
http://www.integratedwa.com

DIGITAL BUSINESS CARD:
http://www.austincollins.org

LINKEDIN:
http://www.linkedin.com/in/proactiveplanning

FACEBOOK:
http://www.facebook/com/proactiveplanning

MARK W. BOSLETT

MARK W. BOSLETT

Conversation with Mark W. Boslett

Mark, you are the founder of Mark W. Boslett, Inc. Tell us about your work and the people you help.

Mark W. Boslett: I'm in three different industries. I own a CPA firm, so I do the accounting and tax work you expect a CPA firm to do. I have clients in 28 different states. I also do business valuations to tell you how much your business is worth. I've been doing that since 2004. Lastly, I've been doing exit planning since 2010. So those are the three segments I cover, and I do a lot of business in each.

*How prepared are business owners
when it comes time to exit?*

Mark W. Boslett: Well, 90% of them have no exit plan, based on Exit Planning Institute surveys. They have most of their money tied up in their business throughout the years and have no idea how to get their cash out of the business. But really, exit planning is about business planning. That's what the Exit Planning Institute would tell you. It would be best to start an exit plan the day you open your doors. It's not about selling the business; it's about growing value so you can sell it anytime. If somebody walks in and offers you money for your business, you're ready to go if you truly want to. Slowly but surely, business owners are starting to understand this.

*What are some common pitfalls
associated with exit planning?*

Mark W. Boslett: The pitfall is when an owner gets an offer, it's about 80% of what they think the business is worth. Every business owner has an idea of how much money they need to retire. But the problem is, if they don't have the value in the business for that number, they will need to change their plans or work longer. Many end up working long past when their passion has run out, so the value of the business just keeps dropping. As a general rule of thumb, not knowing what you don't know is unhealthy.

As we are coming out of a pandemic, is it a good time to sell a business? What have you seen in your market?

Mark W. Boslett: It depends on what industry you're in. There are specific industries that did very well during the pandemic. For example, your business went through the roof if you were selling hand sanitizer. I did a valuation for an event planner, which you would assume didn't go well since there weren't any events during the pandemic. But he found a way to reinvent himself by doing virtual events, and his sales skyrocketed.

Certain businesses like daycares took a hit because nobody was using them. I would say most businesses went down a little bit. But when I'm doing valuations, I don't put much weight on 2020 because it doesn't give an accurate picture of what will happen in the future. When someone is looking at your business, they are interested in buying the future.

Can you give us a 10,000-foot view of the exit planning process?

Mark W. Boslett: It *should* be a painless process, but it depends on your preparation. Suppose you have been trying to grow your business and have been doing very well. It would be best to talk to your advisors three to five years before you exit. Exit planning is all about teamwork, having each advisor in the room to have the same discussion, focusing on their specialties. I can't do everything that has to do with exit planning, but I can do the business valuation. I can value the business and tell you how much it is worth. I don't do wealth management, so I have no idea how to invest your money. I don't want to sell your business, though I have the credentials to sell it. The lawyers do due diligence. You need to make sure your assets and leases are in place, you have done some exit or estate planning, a good marketing plan, and an excellent growth plan so your business can continue to thrive.

As I said, most people are buying the future. Each team member is trying to increase the value of your business. I can tell you what it is worth today, but the exit plan gives you the tools to take it to the maximum potential. When you exit, you can leave at the price you envisioned. You are giving yourself options with an exit plan. If you don't take the proper steps, you won't have many options.

Mark, what inspired you to get started in this field?

Mark W. Boslett: I'm really the number one advisor being a CPA because people always want to talk to their CPA about these things. I met a guy named John Brown in 2007, who was the real founder of exit planning. He is a lawyer, and he talked at a seminar I attended. I got the idea, "If I'm going to help people with taxes, I need to be able to help them with where the money is going. What does their future look like?" It seemed like something the industry needed to have. Sure, I can tell you what your business is worth, but that doesn't do any good if I can't help you get maximum value. I was in the consulting business anyways, and I used to be a CFO for a couple of large companies. So it's all about helping owners get the value out of their business. Most of them have this money tied up, and it needs to be a good investment.

Is there anything else you would like to share with business owners considering exiting?

Mark W. Boslett: When we are talking about an exit, you shouldn't think about leaving. You should think about planning. Planning for an exit starts today or should have started a while ago. You can't decide that you want to sell your business tomorrow or the next day without a plan, which many business owners do. They find they're burned out, and now they want to sell immediately. But that's not when the business is at its highest value. I liken it to selling a house - I don't fix up my house to sell it; I fix it to live in it. You're trying to get the most value out of your business today. The longer you take to plan your exit, the more valuable the business will be. I've been working on my exit for about ten years now since I understood what that meant. I don't know when I'm going to retire. But I know I can and have built value in my business. So think planning, not leaving.

How can people find you, connect with you, and learn more?

Mark W. Boslett: My website is www.markwboslett.com. I have four videos on vimeo.com/markwboslett to give you information about exit planning. You can call me at 330-650-4033 or email me at mark@markwboslett.com.

MARK W. BOSLETT

FOUNDER
MARK W. BOSLETT, INC.

Mark W. Boslett, CPA, CVA, CEPA, CMAP, & CM&AA, has a dual background in both public accounting and a CFO in industry. This skill set makes him unique in the fact that he can give his current clients the same information to help them grow their companies as he did, as the controller of the company, to the President and Board of Directors.

He has experience in several industries, including not-for-profit entities. From 1988 to the present, he has served as president of MARK W. BOSLETT, INC. CPA, provider of financial reporting, tax compliance, and budgeting services for small business clients. He specializes in providing controller-level functions for businesses too small to have a full-time person on staff. He is responsible for personal and corporate tax planning and preparation services. His strengths include the implementation and streamlining of systems that obtain time and cost savings and training of staff to be more effective. This added value to the business he worked for and saved them thousands of dollars over the years.

Mr. Boslett has over fifteen years of experience as a certified business valuation analyst for clients in many different industries and many different states. He is a member of the National Association of Certified Valuators and Analysts. He does business valuations for everything from buy-sell agreements and divorces to mergers and acquisitions and exit planning.

Mr. Boslett has been a member of the Exit Planning Institute, Inc., specializing in Exit Planning for business owners and advisors, since 2010. He is certified to form teams of highly trained professionals and use customized strategies that help business owners exit their businesses with the highest value possible.

Mr. Boslett is a Certified Mergers and Acquisitions Advisor and member of the Alliance of Mergers and Acquisitions advisors. He is certified to help clients buy and sell a business and has been involved in several transactions for clients on both the buy and sell sides, including the purchase of his own business.

Mr. Boslett has served on many different boards of directors and advisory boards. He has served as corporate treasurer for two different companies.

Mark W. Boslett is passionate about small business and wants to help companies become healthy and grow to their full value.

QUALIFICATIONS

Certified Valuation Analyst
Member of the National Association of Certified Valuators and Analysts
Certified Exit Planning Advisor
Member of the Exit Planning Institute, Inc.
Certified Mergers and Acquisitions Advisor
Member of the Alliance of Mergers & Acquisitions Advisors® (The Alliance)

Licensed to buy and sell businesses (has been involved in several transactions for clients on both buy and sell-side, including the purchase of his own business)

EMAIL:
mark@markwboslett.com

PHONE:
330-650-4033

WEBSITE:
markwboslett.com

FACEBOOK:
facebook.com/markwboslett

MICHAEL P. CRAWFORD

MICHAEL P. CRAWFORD

Conversation with Michael P. Crawford

Michael, you are the Managing Partner of enTrust Wealth Advisors. Tell us about your work and the people you help.

Michael P. Crawford: We are a multifamily office serving 80 families and handle everything that has to do with money, from investing to estate planning. Generally, we form teams to help us, but we act as the quarterback for everything that involves finances in their lives. The people we work with have either owned a business in the past, own a business currently, or are retired after selling a business.

LEADING EXIT PLANNING ADVISORS

*How much thought do owners put
into selling their businesses?*

Michael P. Crawford: Usually not enough. They are too busy growing the business over time, figuring out how to cut costs and increase sales. It takes a lot of time to plan how to exit a business, maximize the after-tax take, and accomplish goals.

Business owners often think they don't have the time to sit down, take a step back, and figure out what they want to accomplish. They also believe they can get it done in a few months when in fact, it takes a long time to get a business into a saleable condition.

What are common pitfalls you help business owners avoid?

Michael P. Crawford: One of the biggest pitfalls is not having the accounting situation in great shape. Their books will be analyzed by private equity firms or other potential buyers, so they at least need to have them reviewed by a CPA firm. Before entering the sale process, many business owners just have a bookkeeper and never need a CPA.

The second pitfall is succession planning. Owners need to figure out how their business will run without them in the picture. Most likely, they haven't thought about that before.

Lastly, they have to think about what they will do post-sale. Many business owners sell the business and are left with a lot of time on their hands and no idea what to do with it. There is only so much golf one can play and travel one can do. So they need to understand how much money is required to continue living the lifestyle they want to, and then what they're going to do with all that free time.

Can you give us a 10,000-foot view of how an exit planner helps business owners develop a plan?

Michael P. Crawford: The first thing we do is understand what they're trying to accomplish. If they need X dollars to live every year, we need to figure out how much money after taxes is necessary so that they can meet their financial goals at a decent rate of return. Then we put a team together with the business owner to get the accounting functions in order. If they want to give money to charity or their children, we want to ensure we pass that along efficiently within the context of their goals. So it's really about setting goals, understanding objectives, and getting the right team in place to accomplish those goals.

How did the recent pandemic impact the exit planning industry?

Michael P. Crawford: The pandemic has been a blessing for some businesses and a curse for others. For example, let's look at a mortgage business where the owner planned to exit for a specific number before the pandemic hit. Suddenly, the mortgage business went crazy as the housing situation got out of hand. They processed a tremendous amount of mortgages with these low rates, causing the valuation to increase dramatically. Therefore, we had to strike while the iron was hot and ensure we got everything done quickly to position the business for sale at just the right time. Of course, not all situations are the same, but that's just one specific example.

Michael, what inspired you to get started in this field?

Michael P. Crawford: I got started because I was mathematically oriented. I was interested in investments, estate planning, and the taxation side. I was an accounting major, and I used to be an accountant. So the melding of all of these things was appealing to me. And naturally, business owners are a great target market because they are well off, intelligent, aggressive, and interested in maximizing wealth and being efficient with taxes. So that is how my practice shaped itself.

Is there anything else you would like to share with owners considering exiting their businesses?

Michael P. Crawford: Owners should know the process takes much longer than they think. If they plan to sell their business in a year or two, now is a great time to start putting a team together to help them accomplish their goals. They will most likely need to make changes to the business, hire people to be successors, and clean up the accounting. They may also need to have conversations with children about gifting. My advice is to do things well in advance because a lot of planning is involved.

How can people find you, connect with you, and learn more?

Michael P. Crawford: Our website is www.entrustwealthadvisors.com. We are located in San Diego, California. Our phone number is 858-257-4646, or you can email me at mcrawford@entrustwealthadvisors.com. You can do further research at www.adviserinfo.sec.gov.

MICHAEL P. CRAWFORD, CEPA

MANAGING PARTNER
ENTRUST WEALTH ADVISORS, LLC

Michael is the Co-Founder and Managing Partner of enTrust Wealth Advisors, an SEC-registered investment advisory firm based in San Diego. Michael has been in financial services for over 20 years, specializing in wealth, risk, financial, and exit planning strategies for high net worth individuals and business owners. He is focused on managing wealth to help clients achieve financial confidence and shape enriching lives and legacies.

Prior to founding enTrust Wealth Advisors, Michael spent a combined 16 years at UBS Financial Services and Morgan Stanley focused on helping clients raise venture capital, sell companies, complete large securitized real estate transactions and implement all manner of gifting, asset protection, estate planning, and philanthropic strategies.

Michael graduated from Villanova University with a BS in Accounting. He lives in Del Mar with his wife and two children. He currently serves on the Board of the Exit Planning Institute in San Diego and the CLAS Dean's Advisory Council at Villanova University.

EMAIL:
mcrawford@entrustwealthadvisors.com

PHONE:
858-257-4646

WEBSITE:
https://www.entrustwealthadvisors.com/

LINKEDIN:
https://www.linkedin.com/in/michaelpcrawford/

About the Publisher

Mark Imperial is a Best-Selling Author, Syndicated Business Columnist, Syndicated Radio Host, and internationally recognized Stage, Screen, and Radio Host of numerous business shows spotlighting leading experts, entrepreneurs, and business celebrities.

His passion is to discover noteworthy business owners, professionals, experts, and leaders who do great work and share their stories and secrets to their success with the world on his syndicated radio program titled "Remarkable Radio."

Mark is also the media marketing strategist and voice for some of the world's most famous brands. You can hear his voice over the airwaves weekly on Chicago radio and worldwide on iHeart Radio.

Mark is a Karate black belt; teaches Muay Thai and Kickboxing; loves Thai food, House Music, and his favorite TV shows are infomercials.

Learn more:

www.MarkImperial.com

www.BooksGrowBusiness.com

Made in the USA
Columbia, SC
24 December 2024